IMAGES
of America

UPPER DARBY

Known more recently as the Bond Homestead, the original grant of land was from William Penn to the Kirk family. They erected the farmhouse in 1774 on the eve of the American Revolution. In 1801, the house and 45 acres were passed to Hannah Kirk and her husband, Philip Super. Their daughter Rachael lived there until her death in 1884. Her nephew Vanleer E. Bond purchased 42 acres and the house in 1892. The home and familiar duck pond were located at Lansdowne Avenue and State Road. The Vanleer I. Bond family lived there in 1961 when it was torn down to become the Bond Shopping Center. The site of the pond is now under the bank. (Dorothy Bond.)

ON THE COVER: The newly opened Terminal Building was decorated for a patriotic parade in about 1908. When built, it was praised as the best example of a building used for handling transportation exchanges. Elevated trains, seen in the tunnels, ran from Philadelphia. Passengers then transferred to trolley and bus lines for destinations further west. The vegetable gardens on the left are now the location of the bus terminal. (Upper Darby Historical Society.)

IMAGES
of America

UPPER DARBY

Beverly Rorer and Barbara Marinelli
for the Upper Darby Historical Society

ARCADIA
PUBLISHING

Published by Arcadia Publishing
Charleston, South Carolina

Library of Congress Control Number: 2011925640

For all general information, please contact Arcadia Publishing:
Telephone 843-853-2070
Fax 843-853-0044
E-mail sales@arcadiapublishing.com
For customer service and orders:
Toll-Free 1-888-313-2665

Visit us on the Internet at www.arcadiapublishing.com

Ready for the Thanksgiving Day parade through Sixty-ninth Street are Kathleen Clarke, Beverly Rorer, and Dorothy B. "Debe" Hill who were founders of the Upper Darby Historical Society. They are dressed in original clothing from the early 1900s. This parade took place in the late 1980s. Debe died of lung cancer in 1996, and the society's highest award is named in her honor.

CONTENTS

ACKNOWLEDGMENTS

The Upper Darby Historical Society is fortunate to have a number of skilled researchers and writers among its members. First among those is Thomas J. DiFilippo, author of *The History and Development of Upper Darby Township*. The information from his book and his editing of the historical facts were a significant asset to this production. Another author and researcher is Thomas R. Smith, who wrote *Life in Addingham and Garrettford* and is a walking encyclopedia of information gleaned from his interviews with old-timers.

Our special appreciation goes to the members of the committee who took a chapter and searched for photographs and information to tell their part of Upper Darby's history. They are Kathleen and Robert Clarke, Ellen Cronin, John Devine, Margaret F. Johnson, James P. Manley, and Dr. William J. McDevitt. We are especially grateful to Lori Clark and Laurie Hull McCabe for scanning and formatting most of the images for the chapters in the book. And for a final touch, Mary Ellen Scott was willing to edit all of our writings before we submitted the final copy of the book.

Although most of our images are taken from our own extensive archives, we appreciate Margie Johnson for helping us find images at the Delaware County Historical Society. Robert Seeley, a descendant of both the Sellers and Garrett families, along with Lori Clark, sent extensive materials from their collections. Mark Trickle of Press Publishing was willing to provide us with all the negatives from our historical calendars, and Margaret Mitchell gave us permission to use her collection of photographs. We are grateful to Matthew Nawn for sharing his extensive knowledge of trolleys. Sgt. Timothy Law of the Upper Darby Police Department and David Evans, historian with the Delaware County Firemen's Association, willingly shared their knowledge of their departments. Another wonderful resource was Elizabeth McDonald, chairman of the history department at Upper Darby High School, who let us use a great number of photographs from her files. Unless otherwise noted, all images appear courtesy of the Upper Darby Historical Society archives.

INTRODUCTION

What is a community? Certainly, it is a geographical location—its place on the map—with hills and valleys, streams and plains, as well as forests and open spaces. It is also the structures that dot its landscape—its houses and businesses, churches and schools, government buildings and parks. It is also its paths of transport—its roads and avenues, railroads and trolley lines, perhaps a canal or airport. But most importantly, a community is its people—the young and old, rich and poor, native born and newcomers.

Overlaying a community is its journey through time, its history. Every community has its beginning, its development, and sadly for some, its end.

Upper Darby Township is a community rich in history. The Lenni-Lenapi of the Delaware Nation occupied this area when the first European settlers arrived. In 1655, the Swedes moved up the creeks from the Delaware River. One of the early Swedish cabins remains on Darby Creek and is managed by Friends of the Swedish Cabin.

In 1682, William Penn began selling land grants to his Quaker followers. Upper Darby was settled mostly by English Quakers. Samuel Sellers was the first permanent settler in 1684. As the first wire weaver to arrive in this country, his mills produced wire screens and wool-carding machines. The descendants of the Sellers family contributed much to the development of the country. Prominent among those were two inventions: an early steam engine and the first movie projector.

Another prominent family in Upper Darby was the Lewis family. Ralph Lewis, a Welsh Quaker settler in Upper Darby, purchased the land in 1692 that is now known as Collen Brook Farm. Mary, the last Lewis, married Dr. George Smith in 1829, and he moved into Collen Brook. Soon after, Doctor Smith went to Harrisburg as a state senator. While he was chair of the education committee, the legislature passed the bill establishing public education in Pennsylvania. A most-prominent person, he also wrote a history of Delaware County and helped develop better farming methods. One of the Smith's descendants was secretary of the treasury under President Grant, and another, Ludlow Ogden Smith, married Katharine Hepburn.

During the 18th century, Upper Darby consisted primarily of farmland that produced crops for inhabitants and their animals. In the early 19th century, many turned to dairy farming. The families became quite wealthy, and the area became known as the Butter Belt.

The fall line of the creeks ran through Upper Darby, creating power along the creeks for the early mills. At the end of the 18th century, there were 14 mills ranging from saw and grist to fulling and fabric. Small hamlets grew up around these mills with their own baseball teams and bands.

By 1900, Upper Darby was still a rural area composed of three mill towns—Addingham, Cardington, and Kellyville—and one crossroads village, Garretts Ford. In 1907, however, Upper Darby became a transportation hub with the opening of the terminal building in the Sixty-ninth Street area. It was the end of the line for elevated trains from Philadelphia and the start of interurban trolleys, trains, and buses to the suburbs. This was key to the development of the western suburbs. Sixty-ninth Street was the prototype for shopping areas of its time. Between 1920 and 1930, the population exploded from 9,000 to nearly 50,000.

The largest section of Upper Darby is Drexel Hill, named for the Drexel family. They were wealthy and prominent, owning large estates. One of their daughters became a nun and devoted her life to helping underprivileged children. She donated her inheritance to build schools for "Indian and colored people." On October 1, 2000, she was canonized as St. Katherine Drexel, only the second American to become a saint.

Today, Upper Darby Township has a diverse population of 84,000. The school district is the largest in the state outside of the major cities of Philadelphia, Pittsburgh, and Harrisburg, with 1,000 students per grade. Although mostly Caucasian until the early 1970s, it is now the most ethnically diverse in the state with approximately 80 dialects and languages spoken by students in the high school

The images in this book uniquely capture our history and heritage. From a wilderness settlement to a farming community to an industrial center to a sprawling suburb, Upper Darby has evolved into a thoroughly modern 21st century American community. While we exist in the present, our lives are enriched by remembering and incorporating the roots that brought us to where we are today. We hope that this book will put you in touch with our fascinating past as we look with hope to the future.

One

FARMING AND THE MILLS

After William Penn's Quakers settled in southeastern Pennsylvania in 1682, it soon became one of the wealthiest farming regions in the country. By 1786, the people of Darby and Upper Darby decided to separate for logistic and political reasons.

By 1800, the land was covered with farm fields consisting of grain for livestock feed and human consumption and flax used for linen cloth and oil. But farms needed heavy labor. Well-informed men found better ways of farming, using such practices as new equipment, fertilizers, and crop rotation. In 1840, the invention of the reaper by Cyrus McCormick gave farming a big boost. But by then, most grain farming had moved west. Upper Darby turned to dairy farming, and the families became quite wealthy from milk, butter, and cheese.

Located on the fall line of three creeks, Upper Darby was in a unique position for early settlers looking to build mills. Three creeks run in a southeastern direction through Upper Darby Township: Darby Creek on the western border with Springfield; Cobbs Creek on the eastern border with Philadelphia, flowing into Darby Creek; and Naylor's Run, which flows down the center and joins Cobbs Creek.

This water falling in a short distance quickly provided power to turn waterwheels for mills. Dr. George Smith in *History of Delaware County* listed the elevation of the creeks between 390 feet and 440 feet. So, it was no wonder that the land where water falls from this ridge (a fall line) became the center of early mills. At one point, Upper Darby boasted having 14 mills in its small township.

The first mills were sawmills and gristmills for grinding flour. Other mills were fulling mills for pounding and softening cloth, tanning mills, tilt mills for making cutting edges on knives, linseed oil mills, plaster mills, and paper mills. Textile and paper mills required larger buildings and many workers. The mill owners often built homes for these workers.

Upper Darby people became prosperous and skilled, so the smaller mills were replaced with the larger factory system and Upper Darby became an industrial center by 1850. Some of the mills continued into the early 20th century. The last to close in 1955 was the Kent woolen mill.

Dr. George Brook

John Lewis
SPRING HILL

P. Desmond

E. Leedom

Hannah Bryan

John Kirk

Wm. W. Cotten Clement

Smith w.

Mrs. of C. Lewis

Mrs. H. M.

Levi Lukens

Est. of W. Bryan

John Levis

New State

Road

Jno. Birk

Jon P Eve

Bacon

FERNLAND
Isaac P. Garrett

T. Ring
Hon
Campbe

BLOOMFIELD
Nathan Garrett

Sch'Ho

CLEVELAND FARM
Geo. S. Garrett

Sch'Ho

Hubberd

Joward
Price
Mrs Fielding

Dr. Sharkey

Joseph

HEYVILLE

GARRET FORD
W.P.S.
B.SS.

Garrett Road

Toll Gate

W. Burne

E.
Sharkey

J. M.

Wm S Garrett
W M IO.E
R A Barker
Geo ff Allen
A S Garrett
C Barber
A m Garrett

Jos.
Dunn
Siders
Leighton

Wm
McKirle

Mrs Sarah L Fulton

Anderson

D a
BR

Samuel Hey

Mills

J. & M.
Randolph
Hoffitt
Bro Haley

J. H. Lewis

Randall Bishop

Glenwood
Mills

Jos. Allen

Ester

L. Tackson

John Lobb, Jr.

GLENWOOD

Mills
CLIFTON
Mills

Joel Bishop

Oborn Lewis

Sch'Ho

Darby

George Jones

Falls Run

Friends
M'Ho

J. Ashhurst

CLIFTON

CLIFTON HALL
Est. of Lewis

T. Kent

Union

C A C
CB

Est. of
Kelly

Cobbs Creek

Chester

Dickenson

Est. of Chas Kelly

ClifftonHall
Dr. Robt A Given

Dr. S. P.
Bartleson

Mills

D & C
RR

KELLYVILLE

DAR
ROAD
STA.

Mary H Rhoads

Seth

Lewis

A. H.
Bunting

J. B. Levis

Newton

Sam Clifton

KELLYVILLE STA.

Chas A Wells

HAYBROOK

J. O. Longstreth

CoalYd

CHESTER

KELLYVILLE
Isaac Lobb
Street

Jos. Powell

WEST

GREENBANK
Anne H. Bunting

L. H. B. Jr.
OAKLANE
STA.

Regina
S. G. Levis

CLIFTON
STA.

Sarah Brandt

Geo.
Ash

G. Mill
H. J. Palmer
Upper Darby
Mills

Joshua W. Ash, M. D.

Mrs Anna
Dalmas

Jno Ash,
Est.

D
Bonsall

B.
Bonsall

From Official Records, Private Plans and
Deeds, Surveys of the County Surveyors,
Dr. Ash's Map; the U.S. Coast Survey; and
actual Surveys throughout the County by
HENRY W. HOPKINS, C.E.
Engraved by E. Busch.   J.R.O.Wilmet St., Philad.a

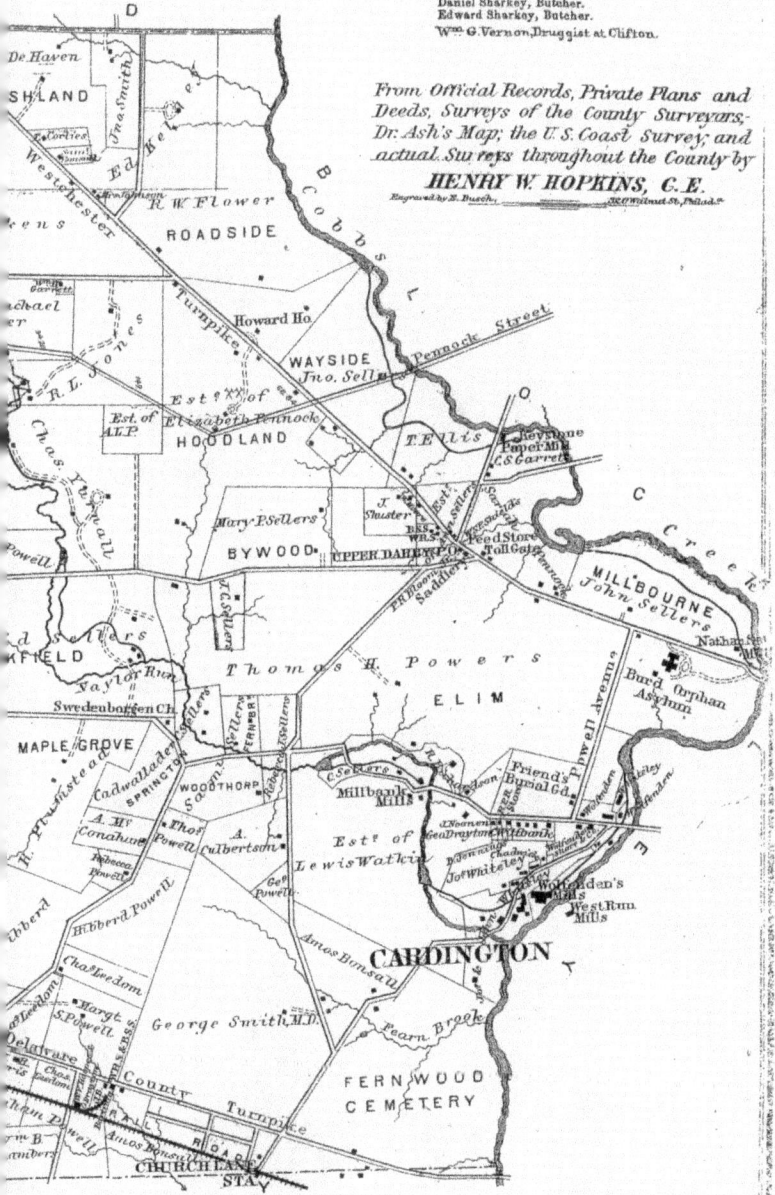

De Haven
SHLAND
Ina Smith
Cortier
R.W.Flower
ROADSIDE
Westchester
Edge
Turnpike
Howard Ho.
WAYSIDE
Jno. Sell
Pennock Street
Est. of Elizabeth Pennock
HOODLAND
R.L. Jones
T. Ellis
Keystone
Paper Mill
L.S.Garrett
J. Stauster
Feed Store
Toll Gate
Mary P.Sellers
BYWOOD
UPPER DARBY P.O.
Chas Yarnall
MILLBOURNE
John Sellers
Nathan
Mill
Powell
KFIELD
Taylor Rice
Swedenborgen Ch.
Thomas H. Powers
ELIM
Burd Orphan Asylum
Creek
MAPLE GROVE
Cadwallader
SPRINGTON
WOODTHORP
Millbank Mills
Friend's Burial Gd.
A. Mc Conahue
Rebecca Powell
Thos Powell
A. Culbertson
Lewis Watkins
Est. of Geo Drayton
Millbank
Geo Powell
Jos Whitelen's
West Run Mills
Wolfenden's Mills
Hibberd Powell
Chas Lee.som
Amos Bonsall
CARDINGTON
Margt S.Powell
George Smith M.D.
Fearn Brook
Delaware
Chas Justice
County
Powell
Turnpike
FERNWOOD CEMETERY
Amos Bonsall
CHURCH LANE STA.

This 1870 map presents a clear view of the dual economy of Upper Darby in the 19th century regarding farming and milling. Note the large size of the land parcels for farms and the number of mill dams and races along each creek. Three swift streams for water power, the proximity to Philadelphia markets, the construction of the West Chester Turnpike, and the West Chester and Philadelphia Railroad all contributed to the strong economic growth of the Township during the Industrial Revolution. For most of the 1800s, Clifton Heights, Lansdowne, Millbourne, and part of Aldan were part of Upper Darby Township.

11

George and Samuel Sellers, natives of Belper, England, arrived with William Penn in 1682 and were granted 100 acres in 1690. The original part of Sellers Hall was built in 1684 and, by 1853, their holdings consisted of 233 acres. The marriage of Samuel Sellers and Ann Gibbons was the first recorded in the Darby Meeting. Their son Samuel was the first of many generations active in the development of mechanical inventions and scientific pursuits. It was John Sellers I, the third generation, who added a gristmill, sawmill, and tilt mill to the property. Below is the parlor of Sellers Hall in about 1908. From 1887 until his death in 1918, Sellers Hall was occupied by William Jones and was one of the first dairy farms to pasteurize and bottle milk.

The Sellers Hall tenant farm, run by Jesse Fullerton around 1900, was located near Long Lane. The wagons are seen in the pasture. In 1922, the land was purchased by the congregation of St. Alice's Parish and Sellers Hall was used as a chapel and residence for the priest.

John Marshall established Millbank Grist Mill by Naylor's Run, west of Sixty-ninth Street. The Nathan Sellers family bought it from John Marshall. Coleman Sellers inherited the mill in about 1834 and built a beautiful summer home next to it. Eventually, Lewis Watkin bought the mill and later gave it to his son William. Watkins Lane and Watkins Senior Center are named for this family. Coleman Sellers, a renowned inventor and manufacturer, married Sophonisba Peale, daughter of the artist Charles Wilson Peale. In 1828, Coleman established a machine factory on Cobbs Creek where his father and uncle had built Delaware County's first cotton mill in 1798. Coleman's company provided machines and machine parts to surrounding paper and textile firms. Machines for carding wool gave the name Cardington to the area. Some of the nation's earliest locomotives were built there.

COLEMAN, SELLERS & SONS,

Engineers, Machinists, & Ironfounders,

Cardington Iron Works.

Office No. 8 North Sixth street, above Market,
PHILADELPHIA.

Locomotive and other Steam
Engines,

Rolling Mills, and all kinds of Mill Gearing; also

Paper Mill Machinery.
MANUFACTURED IN THE BEST MANNER.

Foundry work in general.

Cows from Springton Farm and Brookfield Farm are seen grazing in the meadow by the millrace in about 1912. The two farms adjoined each other along Garrett Road and south of Marshall Road. They were two of 17 plantations owned by the Sellers and Pennock families. Edward Sellers of Brookfield was a captain in the Anderson Calvary during the Civil War, and it was at Brookfield that the Sellers family heard of the assassination of Abraham Lincoln. The water from Naylor's Run flowed to the waterwheel of the tilt mill through a race. The millrace extended from a dam north of Garrett Road through the present site of the Barclay Square Shopping Center.

Millbourne Mills was located at Sixty-third and Market Streets. In 1752, John Sellers, grandson of the original settler, Samuel, established a dam on Cobbs Creek, which still exists today. Below the dam, he built a gristmill operated by waterpower until it became steam operated in 1876. Around 1869, Oliver Evans, the inventor, licensed his automated mill technology to John. By 1885, Millbourne Mills covered several acres and consisted of a storehouse, carpenter shop, blacksmith shop, boiler house, and grain elevators. In 1910, the mills were sold to the Shane Brothers and continued to produce flour until 1921. It was torn down in 1926 to build the Sears and Roebuck Department Store that is no longer standing.

This Millbourne house, pictured c. 1926, was razed in 1939. From 1817 to 1858, John Sellers II occupied the house after it was renovated and enlarged. By the late 1880s, it was part of the Millbourne Mills complex.

This Millbourne Mills wagon seen here c. 1880 is standing in front of the Millbourne house and was from the mill of John and Nathan Sellers. The wagon wheels are wooden with steel rims. The back of the wagon advertises the mill's capacity of 300 bags per day.

KEYSTONE PAPER MILLS.
G. S. GARRETT & SON,
UPPER DARBY, DELAWARE CO., PA.

Office and Warehouse,
13 and 14 Decatur Street, Philadelphia, P

87.47

EY VIEW

Originally on the property of the Keystone Paper Mills were the Sellers' sawmills that created tent poles for the Continental Army during the Revolutionary War. From 1830 to 1854, the mill was used as an oil mill. It was then purchased by Casper Garrett, who substituted machinery to convert it to manufacturing paper. During the Civil War, it produced wrapping paper to package gunpowder used in rifles. It remained in operation until 1928.

CARDINGTON MILLS,
Delaware County, Pennsylvania.

In 1842, John Wiltbanks bought the Sellers' factory, named Cardington Mills. He converted it to a textile mill and later sold it to the Whiteley brothers. They manufactured Kentucky jeans and cloth for military uniforms during the Civil War. In the 1880s, Wolfenden and Shore Company bought the site and greatly expanded it, employing 250 people. Wolfenden, Shore & Company produced military uniform cloth during World War I and finally shut down in 1928. Pictured, James Wolfenden (1889–1949) was president of the Wolfenden Shore Company and resided in Cardington. He was an Upper Darby Township commissioner and served as a US congressman representing Pennsylvania from 1928 to 1947. He served as director of the First National Bank, Clifton Heights and the Sixty-ninth Street Title and Trust Company.

In January 1843, Thomas Kent took over the Union Mill and converted it into a woolen mill. The Great Flood of 1843 destroyed the mill, and Rockbourne (named for the bedrock on which it stands) was erected. It was enlarged in 1850 and modernized in 1921. The Kent Mills closed in 1955.

Tuscarora Textile Factory, nicknamed "Old Tusky," prospered during the Civil War years and, like most of the mills, slackened off production and employment after 1865. The Burnleys sold it to Nelson Kershaw in 1884. After spending his youth as a child laborer in England, George Burnley worked his way up until he was able to buy the ruins of the Palmer & Marker paper mills on Darby Creek in 1844. The mills had been destroyed by the Flood of 1843. He built a cotton and woolen mill and named it Tuscarora. After his retirement, George's son, also named George, took over management of the mill. The Burnley family remained in the Garrettford area until the late 20th century. The family mansion still stands beside Darby Creek and can be viewed from Sycamore Road just south of Garrett Road.

Upper Darby Family Founder

George Burnley
1804 - 1864

Joseph Wilde, seen in the middle wearing a business suit, was photographed with his Tuscarora mill workers around 1900. Notice the young age of some of the workers. Child labor and public education laws were not enforced until Congress passed the Fair Labor Standards Act in 1938. Textile mills were notorious for harsh working conditions. Fourteen-hour days and six-day weeks were the norm. In 1848, the Pennsylvania State 10-hour law took effect. It limited the legal workday to 10 hours and prohibited child labor under 12 years old. However, according to Graham Ashmead in *The History of Delaware County*, the new law did not improve conditions for most Upper Darby factory workers. The law was not enforced and Delaware County factory owners generally ignored the 10-hour law. Below are the Glenwood Mills female workers.

Tenant houses were built and owned by the factory owner. They were usually rented to a family who could provide at least five employees. In Upper Darby, a large family with children of working age (eight years or older) were tenants of mill housing. These homes were situated to the right as one crossed the Rosemont Avenue Bridge from Springfield Township into Upper Darby.

In 1905, Nelson Kershaw purchased 25 acres and a mansion where Palmers Mill Road meets Sycamore Avenue. He owned an additional 65 acres that were later developed as part of Westbrook Park.

"HOODLAND." RESIDENCE OF MRS. DAVID SELLERS. Page 321.

In this c. 1906 photograph, Hoodland, built in 1823 by John Sellers II, is located on State Road. From the front of the house, one could view the Delaware River. In the fall of 1845, Elizabeth Sellers and her husband, Abraham Pennock, moved to Hoodland to care for her ailing father. In 1877, Hoodland was destroyed by fire and rebuilt to its original plan. John Sellers II was a devoted Quaker. His diary tells of abolitionist meetings and visits by poet John G. Whittier.

Abraham Pennock (1786–1868) and John Sellers were agents of the Underground Railroad and ardent abolitionists. Pennock was an editor of the *Non Slaveholder* (1846–1847), a periodical promoting the boycott of all slave-made goods. In 1848, he was the first president of the West Chester Turnpike, and his involvement contributed to the development of the West Chester Pike toll road and, later, the trolley line, which brought significant growth to Upper Darby.

Thomas Garrett (1789–1871) is credited with helping more than 2,700 slaves escape to freedom. Born at Riverview in 1789 to Thomas and Sarah Price Garrett, he moved to Wilmington, Delaware, in 1822. At his funeral in 1871, six former slaves served as pallbearers and carried his casket through the streets of Wilmington to its final resting place at the Friends Meeting House burial grounds.

Robert Seeley, a Garrett descendant, has been portraying his ancestor abolitionist Thomas Garrett since 2005 at more than 100 events. His research was used by the Department of Interior, National Park Service to recognize Fernland Farm as a safe house on the Underground Railroad. (Lori Clark.)

Riverview, pictured c. 1916, was located at Huey and Shadeland Avenues. A stone marker with the initials of "G T & S" and dated 1790 was placed into the chimney stonework when Thomas and Sara Garrett remodeled the original house. This was the original Garrett homestead and home to nine generations of Garretts before it was demolished in 1969 to make way for the School of the Holy Child Jesus.

Fernland was built in 1840 for Isaac P. Garrett (1796–1869) and his wife, Phebe Rhoads. They had no children but raised his nephew Isaac P. Garrett, who remained there until his uncle's death in 1869. Isaac was a teacher at the Eastern School and brother of the famous abolitionist Thomas Garrett. Fernland was a stop on the Underground Railroad. In 1895, Arlington Cemetery was established on this land. (Robert Seeley.)

The Lukens family was among the first Mennonites to arrive in the colonies during 1683. They moved from Germantown to Upper Darby in 1793. Nathan operated a successful dairy and orchard business near Lansdowne Avenue and Cedar Lane. The first section of the typical English-Colonial house was built in 1805. The last to live there was Marguerite. Arthur Sipio converted it to a restaurant, and it is now a computer school.

The old Butler place, for a time, was rented by Nathan Lukens from James Mease. The farm extended back to State Road, the site of Drexel Hill Middle School. Mease's son, Pierce Butler, took the name of his maternal grandfather in order to inherit the property. Pierce married Fanny Kemble, a famous English actress of the day.

Collen Brook Farm was established by the Lewis family, Welsh Quakers, in 1692. It passed to Abraham Lewis III, who built the eastern section in 1794. Their only child, Mary, married Dr. George Smith. The site remained in the family for nearly 300 years until it was purchased by Upper Darby Township in 1989. The farmhouse is listed in the National Register of Historic Places. Pictured at left, the Little Barn, built c. 1710, was converted to a house in 1950.

Dr. George Smith (1804–1882) graduated from the University of Pennsylvania medical department in 1826. He married Mary Lewis in 1829. He was elected to the Pennsylvania State Senate in 1831. In 1832, he was appointed to the education committee, which drafted the Education Act of 1836, guaranteeing children a free education paid for by tax dollars. It still took 20 years for free public education to become mandatory in Pennsylvania. Upper Darby appointed him president of the school board, a position he held for 25 years. He served as a Delaware County judge for many years. In 1833, he cofounded, along with four other men, the Delaware County Institute of Science, now located in Media, Pennsylvania. In 1862, George wrote *History of Delaware County*. He died on March 10, 1882, at the age of 78.

In the 1892 photograph above, Abraham Lewis Smith is seated with his mother, Mary Lewis Smith, on the Collen Brook porch. Mary inherited the property from her parents in 1829. Below, Cheyney Smith Jr., the great-grandson of Abraham Lewis Smith, is standing by the car with his cousins in the driveway of the farm around 1929.

The Eagle Farm (photographed in 1922) was a Collen Brook tenant farm. The small farm was rented by Mary and Martin Pelka, immigrants from Poland. It was bounded by Burmont Road, Stump Lane, and Eagle Road, later named Steele Road. The Pelkas worked the farm until the land was sold for development in 1939. Cheyney Smith Jr. collected the $10 per month rent.

Bunmont Road & TownShip Line   Looking East   Spring 1932

Another tenant farm was known as Flynn Dairy Farm, seen here in 1932 at Township Line and Burmont Roads. Originally owned by Quaker Lewis David, the house was later purchased by the Smith family. The Flynn family rented it for $325 a year and ran a successful dairy farm. By 1925, the house had been abandoned. The land was sold to the Archdiocese of Philadelphia in 1947 and became the location of St. Dorothy's Roman Catholic Church.

Fairlawn was a 90-acre dairy farm that extended for more than 2,000 feet west along Township Line and south to Bond Avenue. Patrick Dermond and his wife, Esther Chambers, became its owners in 1852. Hillcrest School is now located on part of the property known to many people as Llanerch Hills.

Trolley cars collected milk cans from farms along the West Chester Pike route and took them to the Sixty-third Street junction. There, horse-drawn wagons would pick up the milk cans and transport them to markets and dairy factories in Philadelphia.

Two

EARLY NEIGHBORHOODS

Nineteenth-century Upper Darby included Aldan, Clifton Heights, Lansdowne, Millbourne, and East Lansdowne. By 1911, all had separated from the township and created their own governments. The remaining sections became today's Upper Darby Township.

In 1720, less than 20 people owned all the land in the township. By 1800, there were 59 landowners and a population of 862. By 1838, the small villages of Addingham, Cardington, and Kellyville developed around mills along Cobbs Creek and Darby Creek. The village of Garrett's Ford, today's Garrettford, grew up around the major crossroads of Burmont and Garrett Roads.

CHARLES KELLY

Charles Kelly arrived from Donegal, Ireland, in 1821. With the assistance of his uncle Denis, he learned the mill business. After the Great Flood of 1843, Kelly was able to purchase the late Thomas Garrett's mills, 26 acres, a mansion house, and nine tenements. By 1851, he owned 41 tenement homes rented to workers with a population of around 500. The Kellyville Cotton Mill, seen below in the c. 1849 illustration, was located where Baltimore Pike crosses the Darby Creek. Kelly recruited mostly immigrant Irish Catholics who fled Ireland's famine and English persecution only to find conflict and resentment from the Protestants in Philadelphia. Kelly died on March 2, 1864, and is buried in the St. Charles Borromeo Cemetery behind his church. After Charles Kelly's death, his heirs ran the mills until they were sold in 1877. The mills burned to the ground on August 24, 1888.

drawn by C.P. Tholey   Bowen & Co lith Phila

KELLYVILLE.

Seen is the intersection of Market Street (later named Edmonds Avenue) and Garrett Road in the early 1900s. A Scott's Market delivery truck is in the background. Below is the same intersection in about 1930. Deliveries to the Kellyville Rail Station passed along Kellyville Road, later renamed Burmont Road. Michael Blunston held the area's 1682 land charter from William Penn. The property was later acquired by the Garrett family. In 1838, George Garrett laid out the streets and properties creating Market, Randolph, McCoy, and Jones Streets. At the crossroads was a wheelwright shop, blacksmith shop, saloon, barbershop, and Sommer's General Store, later Scott's Market (see page 81). By the 1880s, the village had a druggist, hardware store, baker, candy store, and post office. The annual cattle auction was held behind the saloon.

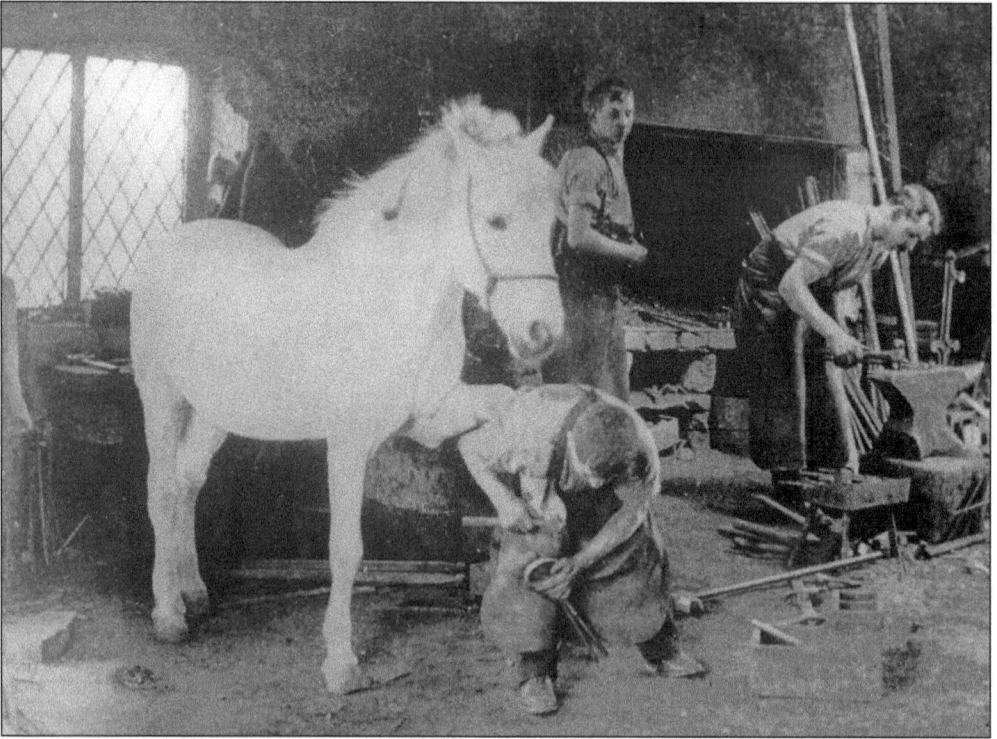

Sam Leaver's Blacksmith Shop (photographed c. 1900) was located on Burmont Road at Garrett Road. The forge is to the right of the window that faced Burmont Road. The blacksmith often acted as a veterinarian, treating hoof problems.

Here is Huey Avenue at Mason Avenue in about 1910. The original Drexel Hill section was developed by Samuel Crothers in 1906. Drexel Heights was built from Bloomfield Avenue to Garrett Road on the western side of Burmont Road. By March 1907, Crothers expanded it to the east side of Burmont Road, north of Garrett Road. The Samuel Crothers sign advertises choice plots and finished houses at reasonable terms.

This is an aerial view of Garrettford from around 1923. The northern part of Burmont Road was a dirt lane winding to State Road, which was also a dirt roadway. In the lower left of the photograph is James Verner's property of 1.5 acres set up with greenhouses for propagating roses. From 1886 to 1895, Verner was the gardener for both Runnymeade and Thorso, A.J. Drexel's summer estates located near Lansdowne Avenue and Garrett Road.

This view of Lansdowne Avenue and Garrett Road was taken sometime between 1914 and 1916. The Lansdowne trolley stop contributed to the development of the surrounding area. Note the gas streetlamp.

Regimental Parade~3°Penna.Inf.-CampA.Merritt Taylor-Upper Darby.Pa.-8-19-17
+ In honor of Brigadier General Sylvester Bonnaffon, Jr +
161A

The Regimental Parade 3rd Pennsylvania Infantry Camp is pictured on August 19, 1917. The estate's property was visited by students of the Drexel Institute, and a civil military training corps was set up under the direction of A.J. Drexel Biddle. By the late 1920s, Riverview (Clarence Fox), Drexel Estate (Harry Koch), and Drexel Park (Thomas Conway Jr. Corporation) housing developments were under construction on portions of the estate.

83.27

The Thurso Mansion is shown above around 1897. By 1892, A.J. Drexel Jr. acquired 36 acres of property on the northeast corner of Garrett Road, across from his father's Runnymede Estate. In 1889, A.J. Drexel Jr. hired the popular Victorian-era architect Wilson Eyre Jr. to build this mansion. In 1898, the house was destroyed by fire and abandoned until the property was sold to the Archdiocese of Philadelphia in 1914. They built St. Vincent's Orphanage, dedicating it on May 9, 1920, and closed the facility in 1952. It was then converted to Archbishop Prendergast High School for boys (see page 110). The only remaining building from the Thurso estate is the carriage house, seen below. This quartered the chauffeur and groundskeeper, and later, it became a dormitory for workers from St. Vincent's Orphanage. It has recently been a fitness center for the high school.

The Runnymede estate mansion is pictured above in the 1890s. In 1850, Christopher Fallon purchased 140 acres and named it Runnymede after his father's home. Fallon built the three-story stone mansion near the southwest corner of Garrett Road and Lansdowne Avenue. It sat high on the hill, surrounded by pine trees imported from Ireland and overlooking a lake on the property. Fallon's widow sold the property to A.J. Drexel Sr. in 1882. A small army of gardeners maintained the property of orchards, walkways, terraced gardens, and elaborate flower beds. A children's playhouse resembling a log cabin and a boathouse were also on the property. Below, the Runnymede mansion lies in ruins after the 1919 fire. In 1919, the property was sold to Harry Koch, a real estate developer.

The Runnymede estate gatekeeper's house was a Victorian gingerbread style. William Leighton, the estate's caretaker, is seen sitting on the porch. Below is the view from the back of Runnymede in about 1900, overlooking what is now Lakeview Avenue. The avenue was named for the lake on the estate. It was filled in, and houses were developed there.

Bloomfield Avenue is in the c. 1900 view above. The Addingham village developed around the cotton mills of Moses Hey and George Burnley. In February 1877, Nathan Garrett filed a charter to subdivide the area for development, calling it the Bloomfield Tract. Later, it was purchased by Henry Taylor and renamed Taylorville. Taylor went into bankruptcy during the Depression of 1870 and sold the mills to Nelson Kershaw, leading to the birth of Addingham in 1875. Below is Bloomfield, the Garrett home, around 1900. The farmland was acquired by the Garrett family in 1736. In 1875, it was inherited by Nathan Garrett, and by 1892, it was sold to become the Aronimink Country Club, later called Hi-Top Country Club. Today, the former Garrett farm is the site of the Drexelbrook Apartments.

This c. 1900 image shows Main Street, now Bloomfield Avenue, in Addingham. There was a local hotel and bar on the left known as the Hog Saloon, which was built by John Howarth in 1870.

Covered Bridge Addingham Pa # 9005

A covered bridge connected the two villages of Heyville and Addingham but was torn down in 1921. A stone bridge is there today. The white building was Lucy Kinsey's store.

In 1828, Coleman Sellers, son of Nathan Sellers, built a foundry known as the Cardington Iron Works. Up until this time, the area was not residentially developed. Many of the mill workers lived in Blockley, which is presently West Philadelphia. The development plans of the Wolfenden and Shore Woolen Mills included the creation of tenement houses for their workers, creating names such as Whiskey Row, seen below in about 1921, and 12 Gun Row. Census records show that by 1900, approximately 400 people resided in the area. In 1928, the mills were closed and sold to the Fairmount Park Commission. The surrounding area was further developed by Louis Zell and Frank B. Rhoads.

This aerial view of Sixty-ninth Street was taken sometime between 1926 and 1928. Thomas H. Powers was one of the township's largest landowners in 1877. Between 1916 and 1926, John H. McClatchy, an enterprising developer, made 67 separate purchases of property in the eastern section of Upper Darby, including most of the Powers estate. McClatchy realized the importance of the Sixty-ninth Street Terminal as a transportation center, and in 1928, he began the development of the Sixty-ninth Street shopping district. Note that in this picture, the Sixty-ninth Street shopping area has not yet been developed. In the left foreground in the triangle is the first municipal building.

By 1930, Upper Darby had a population of 47,145 and was the fastest-growing town in the United States. Eleven transportation lines radiated from the Sixty-ninth Street Terminal (above). It is estimated that 56,000 people and more than 24,000 cars passed it each day. By July 1928, tenants were moving into the Sixty-ninth Street shopping district. One such store was the Frank & Seder Department Store (below).

The University of Pennsylvania's Flower Observatory, seen in this c. 1916 photograph, was dedicated in 1897 and located on the north side of West Chester Pike near Cedar Lane in Highland Park. By 1929, the housing developments of Observatory Hill and Highland Park, built by Wood, Harmon & Co., were well populated. In the 1950s, the observatory closed and was torn down due to increased lighting and smog that made quality observations impossible.

Kirklyn was named after the Kirk family homestead. In the late 1890s, a wheelwright and blacksmith shop were in the area. The sale of the Cunningham farm to Wood, Harmon & Co., part of the Kirk farm to the township's improvement association, and the Kelly farm to the Philadelphia Electric Company for a golf course changed the West Chester Pike landscape.

By 1934, the Depression coupled with real estate taxes forced the Smith family trustees to sell 270 acres of Collen Brook Farm. The farm's quarry was filled in, and the development of the Aronimink Section of Drexel Hill began. This sale allowed the completion of the final portion of the Township Line Road cut-through path to State Road. (James Bierne.)

Three

FUN AND GAMES

The early settlers worked hard to build their farms, homes, and small mills, leaving little time for recreation. The first fun times were probably swimming or fishing in the creeks or ice skating on the frozen ponds.

As the mills were built and villages grew up around them, there was more opportunity for recreation. The mill villagers liked competition between the hamlets. They formed their own bands and participated in parades through the township. The Fourth of July was a popular parade time. They also organized baseball teams and often played on land donated by large landowners.

Clubs formed to satisfy interests. Women joined literary clubs, while children joined a Scout troop or sports group. Later, there were municipal bands and choral groups.

In 1836, Upper Darby School District acquired its first schoolhouse. Once public school districts in Delaware County opened, sports competition was underway between the districts.

In the early 20th century, parades were often sponsored by the local fire departments. Fancy cars and fire trucks were favorite spots in the line of the parade. Children's groups took part later on.

This c. 1914 parade on Marshall Road is coming from Burmont Road and heading toward Shadeland Avenue. The Upper Darby police are seen in the lead of the parade. The policeman on the right with the mustache is Jack Leighton, who, at that time, patrolled the Garrettford section. Leighton also operated a taproom on the corner of Burmont and Garrett Roads.

The spectators watching this Fourth of July parade sit along the 400 block of Shadeland Avenue (formerly Runnymede Avenue). This vintage car is being driven by Arthur Garrett, a descendant of a founding family. He donated the playground at Shadeland Avenue and School Lane for sports and other special events.

This 1918 assembly of children on Park Avenue in Highland Park is parading together. Prior to 1900, children only paraded with their parents or other adults. Notice that the girls are separated from the boys. To the left, behind the small stand, is the Highland Park Fire Company. The Highland Park area was laid out in 1903 as one of the first modern bedroom communities.

Baseball was a very popular activity in the early part of the 20th century. This clubhouse sits on the playing field on Shadeland Avenue. The land was a donation of Arthur Garrett. When an unidentified young girl, who happened to be a talented pitcher, wanted to join the Drexel Hill Borough League, she was rejected. However, Garrett, a Quaker, insisted that she be allowed to play, and she became one of the stars of the team. This game is taking place during 1914.

The Garrettford Citizens Band is shown here around 1904. Garrettford, Kellyville, and Clifton Heights all had community bands made up of men and teens, mostly mill workers and their family members. Below is the Addingham Fife and Drum Corps around 1902. Unlike other local villages, Addingham did not have a community band. Philadelphian Sam Crussin married a local girl who convinced him to come to Addingham and teach music to the children. Money was raised for instruments and uniforms, and the Addingham Fife and Drum Corps was born. It was unique from other community bands because it was made up of only young boys.

Standing on the steps of the Upper Darby Municipal Building, built in 1929, is the Upper Darby String Band in 1936. It was one of several such bands in the area to parade through Sixty-ninth Street. Miss America also marched in the parade that year. Although some local bands marched in the Mummers parade on New Year's Day, only Philadelphia groups could be members of the Mummers.

These ladies are members of a literary club they named the Swastika Club. At the beginning of the 20th century, the swastika was a name and symbol taken from the American Indians, meaning "peace and friendship." They not only met to share famous and original poems, but they also donned uniforms and played instruments in local parades. In the center of the back row is Nina Burnley, whose daughter Nina Dorothy Burnley taught in the elementary schools.

Many will remember the Delaware County Choral Society, directed by Dr. Clyde Dengler. This performance at the Upper Darby Junior High took place on December 14, 1937. The society began before 1929 when Dr. Dengler began his long term as the director. He later served as a Pennsylvania state senator. His son Clyde Dengler Jr. took over as director from 1957 to 1963. In the center of the front row, to the left of the organ, is Vivian Walton who was the accompanist for the society. To the right of the organ is Dr. Dengler. Next to him is Hilda Sanders, director of the children's chorus, which was composed of students from all the elementary schools. They are seated in the top bleachers. To the right of Sanders is Polly Dengler, soloist; David Haupt, who conducted his original work; and Dorothy Grotz, harpist. (Clyde R. Dengler Jr.)

In 1928, the Tower Theater opened as a movie theater and a place for performances. Many classes of Upper Darby High School held their commencement ceremonies in this theater before their larger auditorium was built. In recent years, it has been used for musical performances, particularly rock groups.

In 1948 and 1949, the Ringling Bros. and Barnum & Bailey Circus visited Upper Darby. They disembarked from the circus train at Sixty-third and Market Streets. The entourage followed the elephants down Powell Lane to Marshall Road and then to Sixty-ninth Street. The grounds, south of the intersection, were rented from Wolfenden and Shore Textile Mills. School children were given a half-day off to attend the matinee.

Darby Creek was a popular place for boys to play. The scouts pictured above are standing on a log across Darby Creek. With the leader on the left, they were probably practicing the use of their signal flags. One young boy holds his handbook. In this c. 1918 picture, their uniforms resemble those of World War I soldiers. To the left is a boy playing along the creek in about 1959. He was probably from the Burnley family. Behind them is the Burnley mansion named Tuscarora. The small building is the icehouse, which was torn down in the late 1940s. George Burnley built his house in 1845 when he reclaimed the land after the Great Flood of 1843.

Pictured with Rebecca Hasselman (fourth from the right) are members of her Drexel Hill Riding School. Described by local residents as "going down back hill," Addingham became a popular place for fishing, boating, hunting, and general recreation. On Saturday nights, dances were held on the second floor of the Tuscarora barn.

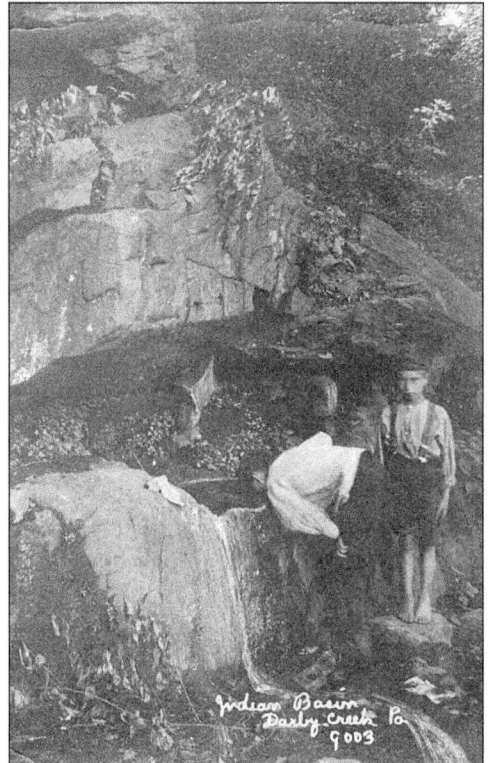

These boys are drinking from an indentation in the Indian Basin around 1906. This is where it was believed that Indian ceremonies were held. It is located on the Tuscarora Tract near Darby Creek. A tiny spring feeds the basin year round. Seen from a distance, the rock resembles the profile of an Indian.

The Aronimink Swim Club, home of the "Green Wave," was originally located at the former central heating plant at Wilde Avenue and Township Line Road. It was organized in 1938 by Wallace Huebner and Paul Rowe. The new swim club was constructed at Dermond and Pontiac Roads. Opening in June 1950, it has been a private swim club since. (Above, Marinelli family; below, Jordan family.)

Eugene Marinelli stands with the Easter Bunny at the swim club in 1989. The Pilgrim Gardens Civic Association has sponsored an annual Easter egg hunt and Christmas tree lighting at the Dermond Circle since 1969. (Marinelli family.)

The Drexelbrook pool, located where the Drexelbrook Corporate Center is today, opened in June 1950. Residents could use the pool even if they were not members of the Drexelbrook Club. It was a popular summertime destination.

Coach Carroll R. McDonald stands in the center of the top row. He guided his young team into the newly formed Scholastic Golf League. Captain Dawson Huber, center of the front row, helped make 1932 a successful year. The team won nine league matches while losing only four and tying one. (Upper Darby School District.)

The 1956 wrestling team won all 10 of its matches and went on to be crowned suburban champions. Four men became district champions and two competed in the state finals. Identified in the image above are Ronald Fordham (far left, first row) and Robert Costagliola (third from left, first row). Coach Peter Bernadino is on the far right. (Upper Darby School District.)

For many years, the Upper Darby Rifle Team had a reputation of excellence, and in 1956, it finished the season undefeated, becoming the district and regional champion. Led by captain Anthony Geno (second row, fifth from left), the team placed third in the state. Charles Wood (second row, third from left) was the advisor. (Upper Darby School District.)

This 1968 Monsignor Bonner High School football team had a very successful season in the Catholic League. Seated fourth from the left in the first row is John Cappelletti. From high school, Cappelletti went to Pennsylvania State University where he broke a record with four touchdowns in two straight games and the most yards run. At left, Cappelletti holds his 1973 Heisman trophy with his brother Joey. During this time, Joey had leukemia and once ran a high fever that put him into a coma. He survived but struggled with his health every day. John and Joey were very close. Joey frequently demanded that John make a certain number of touchdowns in a given game, and John met his requests. At the trophy ceremony, John made an emotional acceptance speech and dedicated the trophy to Joey. The movie *Something For Joey* soon followed. Joey died in 1976. (Anna Cappelletti.)

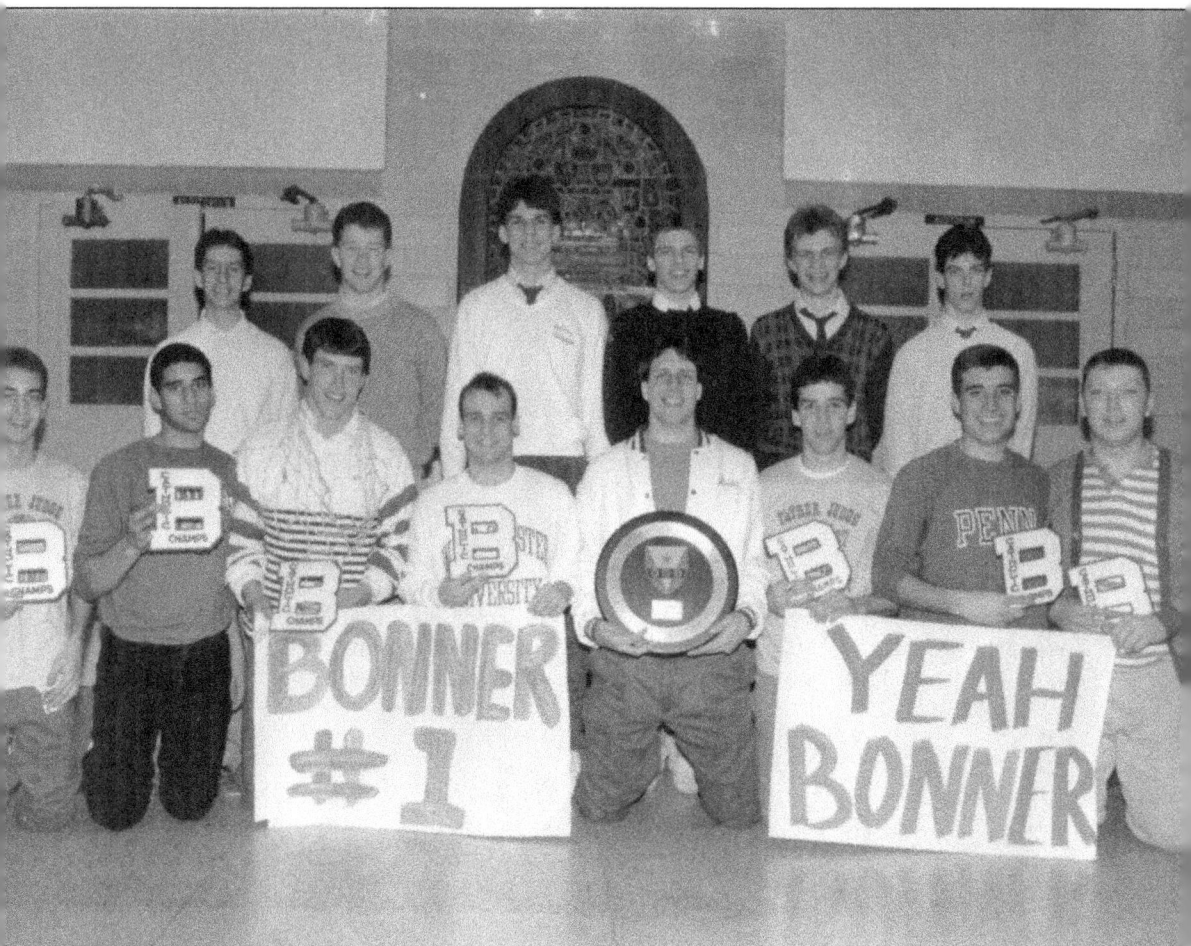

In 1988, Monsignor Bonner High School won the Philadelphia Catholic League basketball championship. Pictured from left to right are (first row) Bill Ciaverelli, Sam Franklin, Dan Summers, Ron Zuccato, Brian Daly (holding the championship Plaque), Fran George, Ted Mulroy, and Charlie Carbin; (second row) Eric Burke, Pat Lynch, Tom Fitzpatrick, Jeff Tinari, Jim Stinger, and Brian Reagan. Brian Daly was the recipient of the 1988 Markward Award as the best high school basketball player in the Philadelphia area. (Brian Daly.)

The Drexel Hill Church Players began their fall performances in 1984. Anita Baker was the organizing force for the programs. In this 2008 performance of *Cinderella*, Mark Watter is the prince and Ali Caizzo is Cinderella. There has been more effort lately to involve the community and tie in with Summer Stage. The producer for the last six years has been David O'Connell. (David O'Connell.)

Summer Stage, established in 1976 by Harry Deitzler, is an award-winning children's theater program at the Upper Darby Performing Arts Center. This is a scene from *Grease* featuring actress and writer Tina Fey as Frenchie, one of the Pink Ladies. Harry received the Barrymore Award–Lifetime Achievement Award in October 2011. (Donald Fey.)

Four

MODES OF TRAVEL

At the beginning of the 20th century, with the exception of trolleys on West Chester Pike and the railroads running through Fernwood, people still depended on horses or horse-drawn carriages for transportation. There were approximately 100 homes in Upper Darby, and most of the area was still undeveloped farms and pastures. The West Chester Traction Company operated its trolleys from Sixty-third Street in Philadelphia to West Chester, but most people could not afford the ride. Its terminal building, which accommodated the extended elevated Market Street train system to Sixty-ninth Street, was opened in 1907. With the terminal in place as a hub, developers anticipated the trolley system that would be constructed to make all the township areas accessible. This made Upper Darby convenient to downtown Philadelphia, stimulating the purchase of land and development of the Sixty-ninth Street area, Stonehurst, Highland Park, Observatory Hill, Kirklyn, Bywood, Beverly Hills, Drexel Hill, Garrettford, Clifton Heights, and points west. As quickly as homes were built, they were sold to people who wanted to live in a suburban atmosphere but have access to center city Philadelphia. The transportation system led to a population growth from 5,385 in 1910 to 56,882 by 1940.

The c. 1900 picture above shows the Young family out for a drive. Howard and Emma Sommers Young are with their children, Anna Cora and Emma Mead, as well as a grandmother. They are facing east on Garrett Road at Shadeland Avenue. Both carriages show similar four-wheeled, front seat and back seat buggies with pull-down windows. The carriage above is powered by one horse, and the carriage below, with one of the Sellers men at the helm, is pulled by two horses. Shortly to give way to the automobile, the horse and carriage was the principal mode of transport for those with the resources. A few years after these pictures were taken, access to the new trolley system led to the demise of the horse and carriage.

This wonderful photograph of an open-air summer trolley car was taken around 1905 near the terminus of the West Chester trolley line. It plied between Sixty-ninth Street and West Chester. It was one of five cars used by the line to take passengers to Castle Rock Park, near Edgemont, for fun and picnics. A sprinkler car went ahead to spray water on the tracks and keep down the dust.

This trolley sits at the Clifton station in 1907. It was the end of the line at Baltimore Pike. This car, No. 21, was planned to run in units so it had open doors between cars and hinged trap doors above the steps to fit the platforms. The tracks later extended to Aldan and, by 1914, to Sharon Hill.

The Sixty-ninth Street Terminal, with its robust Romanesque-style brick facade facing West Chester Pike, was built in 1907. The terminal made Upper Darby the public transportation gateway to Delaware County and beyond. The tracks in the foreground belonged to the West Chester Traction Company; in 1898, they ran from Sixty-third Street out West Chester Pike to West Chester. The tracks were later moved to the rear of the terminal. At the completion of construction, the Sellers and Pennock families granted a right-of-way through the village of Millbourne, and the Market Street elevated train line was extended from West Philadelphia to the terminal.

The 1916 photograph above looks out over West Chester Pike from Sixty-ninth Street. On the right side of the highway is toll house No. 2 across from the State Road trolley station. Note the fields on the right as State Road ended at West Chester Pike. The home of John Sellers (1762–1847), known as Wayside, is on the left. Most of the wires on the multitiered poles carried telegraph messages rather than phone conversations. Below, tollgate house No. 2 is seen from the front. A long pole called a pike was swung across the road. Travelers would call for the gatekeeper to turn the pike so they could pay their toll and pass through. Thus, the word "turnpike" was born. The toll, ranging from 1¢ to 5¢, paid for repairs to the original plank road.

The above 1911 eastbound view of West Chester Pike at Cedar Lane shows the trolley stop and tracks on the right and West Chester Pike to the left. Cedar Lane is the oldest of the perpendicular streets into a main thoroughfare. Built around 1740, it connects West Chester Pike with Darby Road (now Lansdowne Avenue). Below is another view facing west over the area in the 1930s.

Trolley No. 15 of the Chester & Media Electric Railway Company, was the first electric trolley car to operate in Media on April 3, 1893. By the late 1930s, the Philadelphia and West Chester, then part of the Red Arrow Lines system, became the last electric trolley line to serve Media. It remains in operation today as part of the Southeastern Pennsylvania Transportation Authority, commonly known as SEPTA. (Delaware County Historical Society.)

This Clyde Eichholtz photograph of the Shadeland Avenue trolley stop shows the trolley going toward the Sixty-ninth Street Terminal. Notice the Victorian clothing on the people at the platform. This stop was referred to as the Media Junction at Shadeland Avenue. The area was known for picnics in the summer and a community Christmas tree in the winter; thus, the saying "Meet me at the Media Junction" was coined.

E. Clyde Eichholtz was an amateur photographer who moved to Drexel Hill in 1911. He hung out with local pillars of the community and took his camera to record special events and buildings under construction. In the above picture, Clyde has set the timer on the camera so he could jump back into the photograph. However, he was late getting settled, hence the blurry figure in the center. Below are family and friends in Eichholtz's 1917 Buick touring car. Seated on the running board are friends Jan and Frank.

Another favorite means of travel was by bicycle or motorcycle. Here are two prominent brothers on their motorcycles. Lawrence M.C. Smith is on the left with brother Ludlow Ogden Smith. Lawrence is still wearing his dancing pumps from the night before. Not only did Lawrence preserve Collen Brook Farm in Upper Darby, but several other historical sites as well. Ludlow married Katharine Hepburn in 1929. (Eleanor Smith Morris.)

In the 19th century, besides farming and milling, the third-largest business was stone quarrying. This truck of George Burnley was used c. 1920 to haul stone from the quarries in the area. One quarry belonged to Dr. George Smith of Collen Brook. It was at the southeast corner of State and Burmont Roads. The other was on Township Line near Lansdowne Avenue. Note that this is a chain-driven Mack truck.

This is a rare sight on Garrett Road across from Naylor's Run Park in 1936. This streamliner was on display on the public carload siding of a track not in use since 1907. The train consisted of an engine, coach, diner, Pullman sleeper, and a rear observation car. It introduced a modern air-conditioned train to the commuting public. (Pennsylvania Railroad Technical and Historical Society.)

This scene shows car No. 83, a 1932 product of the J.G. Brill Company. These were the first high-speed, lightweight cars acquired by the Philadelphia and West Chester Traction Company. They were ideally suited for use on the West Chester and Media lines because there were long stretches of right-of-way. The cars' relatively low electric consumption and one-man operation helped them survive the Great Depression.

In 1943, the Red Arrow's Llanerch Bus Garage contained a completely equipped machine shop where bus engines and trolleys were regularly checked and overhauled. Spare parts for every type and make of engine in the fleet were in stock. Below, snow sweeper car No. 5 was built in 1920 and purchased by Red Arrow in 1940 from New York State Railways. Two circular brooms are visible on each end. When rotated, they would blow the snow off the tracks. The car was much newer than sweeper No. 3 behind it, which was built in 1912. They would have been taken out of storage and checked in the Llanerch garage in preparation for winter snows.

This interesting c. 1926 view of Sixty-ninth Street shows West Chester Pike with Victory Avenue going off to the right. There are still some horse-drawn wagons among the cars and trucks. The building in the center is the train control tower; the lower part still exists. A subway–elevated train can be seen on the right in the turnaround.

Looking East on West Chester Pike, this 1930 view shows the back of the terminal building where the trolleys would enter to drop off and pick up passengers. Two Red Arrow buses are loading at the bus lane adjacent to the Sixty-ninth Street Terminal. The buses were effective feeders to the rail lines, making them a lucrative method of transportation. In 1937, two companies were combined to form the Red Arrow Lines. (Delaware County Historical Society.)

Five

THE EVOLUTION OF BUSINESS

In the early days of Upper Darby, business consisted mainly of small family shops. These ranged from cigar shops to farm feed stores. Farms in the area changed from raising mostly grain to cattle products and dairy farms. This took place in the early 19th century when roads improved enough to carry their products in wagons.

Family-run stores grew in size and number. Each area of the township had its own stores so residents could have convenient shopping. Several stores provided home deliveries and a credit system for regular patrons. With the introduction of electricity, the creeks lost their importance for power to the mills, and with the closing of the mills, no industrial plants took their place.

Beginning about 1910, several businesses adapted to the changing times and needs of the community. Blacksmith shops became auto repair shops. Family stores gave way to shopping centers. Upper Darby boasted of one of the first hospitals and public libraries in suburban Philadelphia.

Completion of the passenger terminal building at Sixty-ninth Street in 1907 and the extension of the trolleys into and through Upper Darby brought a sharp rise in housing development, small businesses, and population. From the terminal, trains, trolleys, and buses carried people to the housing developments within Upper Darby and to the suburbs further west. In 1910, the population was about 5,800. It grew to 47,145 in 1930, making it the fastest-growing township in the country. Its population peeked at 94,000 in the early 1970s. John McClatchy, a developer and builder, saw the importance of the changes and, in the 1920s, began developing the Sixty-ninth Street area. It became densely populated, and he made what became the country's first and grandest outdoor shopping mall—a revolutionary concept at that time. He was able to sell as many as 168 still-to-be-built homes in a single day. By 1930, Upper Darby ranked second to Philadelphia in retail sales. Today, the tax base is made up primarily of businesses in the Sixty-ninth Street area, strip and shopping malls, and the residents.

In 1810, Abraham Pennock built the Howard House as a temperance inn to accommodate travelers who opposed the use of alcohol. Pennock was an avid supporter of the abolition movement, helping many slaves to freedom. His house was well known to the slave engineers as one of the stops on the Underground Railroad, and he never lost a slave. This establishment also served as a stagecoach stop and post office. In 1916, it was remodeled as the Pennock Apartments. Its last use was as a florist shop before being torn down in 1973 to make room for Pica's Restaurant and a parking area on West Chester Pike at Pennock Avenue.

The Fernwood Masonic Hotel stood on the southwest corner of Baltimore Pike and Church Lane. The first two floors housed stores and a hotel. The Masonic Lodge occupied the top floor. It was frequently called the Fernwood Hotel and accommodated commuters from the city and summer guests escaping the heat and diseases of Philadelphia. Note the trolley tracks on Baltimore Pike.

On West Chester Pike at Garrett Road stood this little cigar store. The proprietress can be seen standing on the porch. The store sold shoes and a brand of cigarettes known as Sweet Corporal, which included trading cards in the pack—a very popular item at the time. On the right is the Bond Feed Store with a sign advertising Arlington Cemetery. Note the West Chester Pike trolley tracks.

Vanleer E. Bond, born in 1848, married Martha in 1876 and started this feed business at what is now the southwest corner of Garrett Road and West Chester Pike. It later became the site of the Sixty-ninth Street Theater and is now apartments. The tracks on the right run down West Chester Pike. The Millbourne Hotel can be seen on the right, and the trolley and subway terminal is to its right.

The first store at this location was built by William King in 1865. Later, Joseph Sommers, seen above standing on the porch, was the storekeeper of Sommers Market. It was one of Upper Darby's first post offices and jails. The Sommers estate sold it to William J. Scott in 1910. The photograph below shows Scott's Market with the truck used for deliveries. By the late 1920s, horse-and-carriage deliveries were replaced by motorized trucks. Generations of Garrettford families patronized the shop, which offered personalized delivery service and credit to customers. The building was demolished in October 1986 for a Wawa convenience store.

The Clark Store, on the corner of Edmonds Avenue and Marshall Road, was a family legacy spanning six generations. Several Clarks served as firemen with the Garrettford Fire Company. Frank Clark was the first in the area to own a car. Russell Clark picked up produce at the dock with his blind horse. The store also served as a post office. Today, the building remains a home but without the porch. (Clark family.)

Built by Thomas K. Manley in 1873, this store was at 100 West Baltimore Pike at Sycamore Street in Clifton Heights. It was operated by Katherine and her brother Joseph, the two adults in the photograph; Katherine is in the doorway. Their store was one of the first homes on Baltimore Pike to have electric lights. It was a stagecoach stop on the Philadelphia-to-Media run and then a trolley stop. It still stands today. (James Manley.)

Penman's house furnishings store was located on West Chester Pike and Linden Avenue. Charles Penman, pictured, bought the new store in October 1923. It operated from 1924 to 1937. The adjoining stores are Gillespie's meat market and the Greater Atlantic and Pacific Tea Company. Note the two gas pumps and the black oil pump on the sidewalk, both a bit unusual for this type of store.

Vanleer I. Bond opened his service station in 1927 at State Road and Lansdowne Avenue. It was across from the Bond Homestead. In 1962, the home was replaced by the Bond Shopping Center. Roger Rossi recalls that in 1928, Vanleer took him in and let him live upstairs for six years. He sent Roger to school at Goodyear Tire Company so he could sell tires for him. (Dorothy Bond.)

On June 24, 1927, the Delaware County Memorial Hospital opened. It was built on land donated by Thomas Conway, whose farm had covered this land and all of Drexel Park. His son Thomas Conway Jr. was made president of the hospital. On opening day, he accepted an ambulance donated by American Legion Post No. 214. Notables in attendance were Arthur H. James, lieutenant governor of Pennsylvania, and Dr. Theodore B. Appel, Pennsylvania secretary of health. This first hospital had only 56 beds. Below, a nurse accepts the donation of an ambulance from two ladies representing the Junior Aid of the Junior Auxiliary Volunteers in 1940. Since then, the hospital has grown with nearly 5,000 patients per year requiring hospital transport. In 2006, the newly renovated and expanded emergency department opened. The 10,000 square feet of additional space more than doubled the previous emergency department. (Above, Keith Lockhart; below, Delaware County Memorial Hospital.)

In 1859, Dr. Robert Given built Burn Brae as a private hospital for patients with mental and nervous diseases and alcohol and drug habits. The grounds covered 58 acres, stretching from Oak Avenue to Bishop Avenue, and included a lake and dairy farm. Patients could stroll the woodland paths and meadows with peacocks and various other animals that roamed the property. The property's lake was located where Home Depot is today. The land was sold to build the Bazaar of All Nations in 1960.

THE BURD ORPHAN ASYLUM OF S! STEPHEN'S CHURCH.

Ca. 1863 – 1920

The Burd Orphan Asylum was established in 1856 by Eliza Howard Burd. The asylum opened in 1863 at Sixty-third and Market Streets and featured early Gothic-style architecture in the shape of a Greek cross. In 1920, the property was purchased to construct an amusement park, but the idea was later abandoned. In the early 1930s, the building was razed for a new housing development.

St. Vincent's Orphanage was dedicated on May 9, 1920. The home housed girls ages three to 18 and preschool boys. At its peak, the home housed as many as 500 children and was operated by the Sisters of Charity and funded by the Archdiocese of Philadelphia. The orphanage closed in 1953 and was relocated to St. Davids, Pennsylvania.

Known as the Cardington Spur, this site at Sixty-third and Market Streets was where the Cardington Railroad spur ran under Market Street to the Sellers Millbourne Grain Mill. It serviced Kunkel Coal on the right. Next to Kunkel Coal is the Derr Lumber Company, and the wall of the Burd Orphanage is seen on the right. These mill areas gave rise to many small businesses.

The Beatty Lumber and Millwork Company has operated in the same location since 1923 when C.H. Beatty and C.R. Owens were co-owners. In 1955, Harper Beatty took over. Since 1999, his grandson Eric Tucker has served as general manager. Supplies were loaded by hand, then by forklift starting in 1967. Their business continues despite a destructive fire in 1970 and a flood in 2004.

In this aerial view of the Sixty-ninth Street area is the terminal building with the trolley sheds in the center. Notice how few buildings there are along Sixty-ninth Street in the upper right corner of the picture. In the foreground is the loop for the elevated trains. To the left are the car barns and the power plant smoke stack. To the right of the terminal is the McClatchy Building under construction, and in the photograph below is the completed McClatchy Building. Starting in 1916, John McClatchy made 67 separate purchases of land. The Powers estate was bought for $6,000 per acre, and 15 years later, the Market Street frontage sold for $2,800 per foot. The McClatchy Building, faced with colorful ceramic tiles, was built and owned by John McClatchy in 1926.

This Drexel Hill Title and Trust Company with an adjoining post office was built in 1923 at the corner of Shadeland Avenue and Garrett Road. During World War II, ration stamps were distributed from this site. The bank closed its doors during the Depression. The building is now the Spencer T. Videon Funeral Home. The Givnish family bought the funeral home in 1986 but maintain the Videon name.

Pyle & Innis was founded by William Pyle and Jack Innis in 1933. The first location was in the garages of the Videon Funeral Home, seen above. It moved down the street to the current location at 3421 Garrett Road in 1939. Prior to moving in, this building had been used as a morgue. The police used the basement as a lounge when they were on foot patrols before they had vehicles.

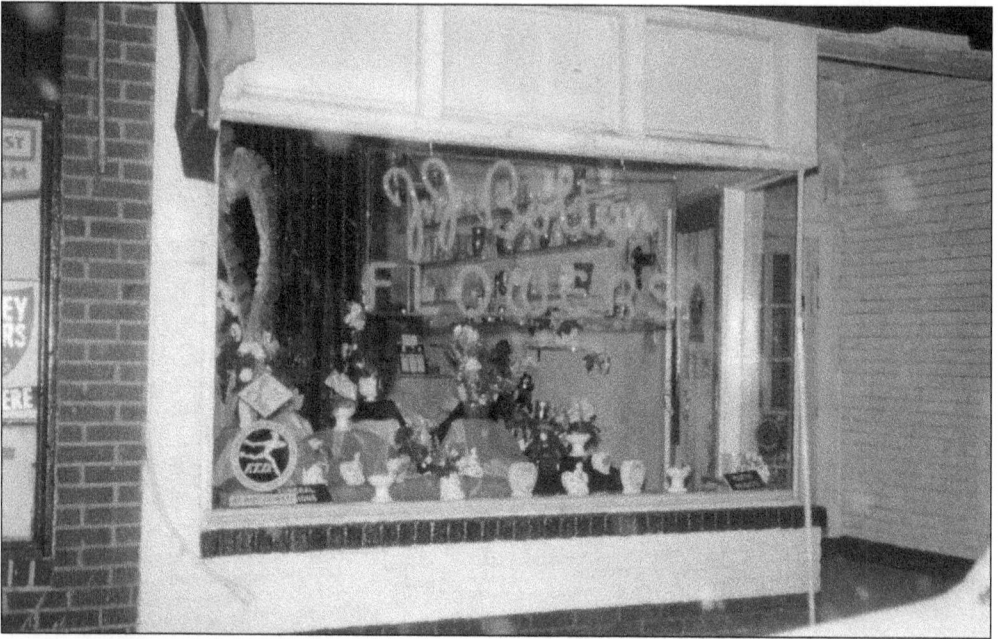

The Bolton Flower Shop at 647 Long Lane was operated by John J. Bolton from 1947 until his death in January 1971. This photograph was taken in 1958. Most businesses in the Stonehurst Hills section of Upper Darby were family owned and operated. (Joseph Bolton.)

John's Seafood Restaurant was located at 657 Long Lane in Stonehurst Hills. This is a section of Upper Darby nearest to Philadelphia. The restaurant opened in the early 1960s and operated for about five years. (Joseph Bolton.)

In the 1940s, the Sunset Restaurant was a popular place for dinner before a movie. After World War II, there was a rise in memberships in service clubs. These clubs would often have their special dinners here. It was located at the corner of West Chester Pike and Pennock Avenue, now the site of a Wawa convenience store.

This 1936 picture shows employees in the Parkhill Family's Meat and Grocery store on Burnley Lane in Drexel Hill. You can see some of the advertised prices for the foods. A close examination reveals some prices on the shelf edge of 50¢ or 60¢ for the items on that shelf. Note the old cash register and other earlier model equipment on the counters. (Mary Ellen Scott)

This farmers market was in the Stonehurst section of Upper Darby at 655 Long Lane. Bernard Levin is standing in front of his market. He owned the store with his brother Samuel from 1953 to 1959. These markets were popular to those living in these smaller neighborhoods. (Joseph Bolton.)

Along the main court of the pedestrian walkway in the Sixty-ninth Street Terminal were a number of businesses. The view above looks down the twin tunnels toward the trolley and bus platforms. The terminal shops were a great convenience for people hurrying home to pick up something between the elevated trains and the Red Arrow Lines. The usual wait for the next transit left time to shop. One may recall these 1942 styles. Liggett's was a shortcut to Market Street. It later became Sun Ray Drugs. The glass doors under the sign with the clock were the exit doors from the Terminal Theater. Below is the meat counter where the main course was purchased for that night's dinner.

Many will remember the days of the milkman, recalling the clank of glass milk bottles as he delivered milk directly to one's door. The cream would rise to the top of the bottle and was skimmed off to make whipped cream. Before there were trucks, local dairies such as Crawford's delivered milk by horse and wagon. Below is a Turner and Westcott truck. (Below, Margaret Mitchell.)

Six

EARLY CHURCHES AND SCHOOLS

Religion and education have always been important elements in the fabric of Upper Darby Township. William Penn, a Quaker, established the colony of Pennsylvania in order to escape religious persecution by the Anglicans in England. In reaction to this persecution, Penn signed his Charter of Privileges in 1701, granting to Pennsylvania colonists, among other rights, the free exercise of religion. Thus, Pennsylvania became a magnet for people of faith from every religion and creed. For example, until the Revolutionary War, Pennsylvania was the only territory in the entire British Empire in which a Catholic Mass could be said legally. Upper Darby embraced religious freedom, and it is reflected today in the many houses of worship that represent virtually every major religion known to man.

In addition to religious freedom, Upper Darby was at the forefront of education. Dr. George Smith, a resident of Upper Darby, chaired the Pennsylvania State Senate Education Committee that wrote the act bringing public education to the commonwealth in 1836. Despite fierce resistance from landowners who would pay the property taxes to support the public schools and from religious schools, which feared the competition for students, both public education and private education have flourished in the township. Upper Darby Township has one of the largest public school systems in the commonwealth, while many religious and secular private schools also coexist in the township. Many graduates of Upper Darby schools have gone on to accomplish great things, and they have left their mark for the better on both the community and the nation.

Saint Charles Roman Catholic Church, the first Catholic church in Upper Darby, was built by Charles Kelly in 1849. This original church seen here was dedicated on October 13, 1859, and seated 450 people. The first resident pastor was Fr. John Shields. This building was demolished in 1890, and the present church was completed in 1892.

James Robinson, an operator in the Clifton Mills, was a preacher in the Swedenborgian Church in England. He preached his first sermon in the picker room of Kent's Mills in Kellyville. The cornerstone of this church was laid in 1830 on Levis family property on Marshall Road near Naylor's Run. Many Upper Darby families were members of the congregation. A number of Quaker families joined after being "read out of meeting," or excommunicated. It was demolished in 1912.

This Drexel Hill Baptist Church, built in 1908, is located on Garrett Road between Edmonds Avenue and the trolley tracks. The Reverend Lynn Drake took his first assignment there as the first minister. He was beloved by all and known as the "Little Minister of Drexel Hill." The building was sold to the Church of the Brethren, a denomination established in 1708 in Germany. In 1964, a large education center was added.

In 1832, a society of Methodists organized in Upper Darby. In 1837, Mt. Pleasant Methodist Church was built at the foot of Garrett Road. In 1923, members of Mt. Pleasant Methodist Church and Broad Street Methodist Church of South Philadelphia merged. The cornerstone for the first part of the present church was laid in 1923 at Burmont Road and Bloomfield Avenue. Since 1968, it has been known as Drexel Hill United Methodist Church. (Drexel Hill United Methodist Church and Margaret Dimmler.)

The children of Christ Presbyterian Church gathered in 1928 to celebrate Children's Day. This building was dedicated on October 17, 1926. The present American Colonial–style church opened in 1942. It occupies the entire block on State Road between Turner and Foss Avenues. In 2010, it was sold to the Beulah Tabernacle Congregation. (Rev. Clyde E. Griffith.)

On May 23, 2010, the congregation of Calvary Presbyterian Church merged with Riverview Presbyterian Church. Calvary Church was established in 1908, and the building was completed in 1928 at Pennock and Wayne Avenues. The combined congregations use the Riverview Church (seen here between 1914 and 1916) at Garrett Road and Riverview Avenue, which is now Calvary Riverview Presbyterian Church. This image shows the first one-story structure before the later additions. Note the gas streetlamp on the corner.

The Sellers Memorial Church was built on State Road and Sellers Avenue across from the Sellers' home, which later became Sellers Memorial Library. In this picture is Sarah Sellers in the black hat at the cornerstone ceremony in 1927. Today, the church is known as the New Life United Methodist Church.

The Church of the Incarnation Episcopal Church was founded in 1915. The first building was constructed in 1919 and the rectory was soon added. It was further enlarged in 1929. The first full-time priest was the Reverend Edward G. Knight. This early picture shows the use of folding wooden chairs before the pews were made. In 1973, the church merged with Holy Sacrament Church on West Chester Pike. (Incarnation Holy Sacrament Episcopal Church.)

The Crossroads Community Church was founded by Dr. Edward Anderson in 1883. Members first met at Mrs. McCallum's home on West Chester Pike near Keystone Avenue. The growth of the church was so rapid that in the summers, they met in a tent just east of Sixty-ninth Street. During Easter Sunday on April 17, 1927, the laying of the cornerstone of the building was celebrated, and the first service was held on June 12, 1927. (Below, Crossroads Church.)

Saint Andrew's parish was established in 1916. Fr. Joseph McShain, the first pastor, outfitted a house at Berry Avenue and Burmont Road with a chapel. A year later, he built a frame chapel that fronted Foss Avenue at School Lane. A combination school and chapel replaced the frame church in 1922. The current church, pictured here before the roof was raised in 1963, was built in 1928. (St. Andrews Church.)

The Reverend Joseph P. Duross, a recently returned Army chaplain, was appointed founding pastor of the newly established parish of St. Dorothy. Mass was celebrated on Christmas Day during 1947 in this new first church, which was built on 8.5 acres at Burmont Road and Township Line Road. Mass was celebrated in the new and present church on Palm Sunday in 1961. (St. Dorothy Parish.)

Grace Evangelical Lutheran Church at 600 Edmonds Avenue opened its doors in September 1926. As early as 1912, plans were made to organize a Lutheran congregation in Drexel Hill, but it would be 11 years before a congregation was formed and another three before the church building could be constructed and opened. In the mid-1950s, a new education wing facing Edmonds Avenue expanded the church to its present size. (Charles Landry.)

Temple of Israel, the first and only synagogue in Upper Darby, was established in 1944 by a group of women headed by Rosalyn Kessler that decided to form a sisterhood. The Publicker family donated the land on Bywood Avenue and the cornerstone was laid in 1950. In 1999, Cantor Sam Appel celebrated its 55th anniversary. The doors closed as a place of worship on July 1, 2002. (Temple Israel and Elaine Cohen.)

The Union School, erected in 1833 on land donated by Coleman Sellers, sits on Marshall Road near the Quaker Burial Grounds in this 1908 photograph. When the Public School Act of 1836, authored by Dr. George Smith, was passed, the building became part of the Upper Darby School District. It operated until 1894. The oldest-existing school building in Upper Darby, it now operates as an automobile repair shop.

In 1869, the first formal parochial school in Delaware County, St. Charles, opened its doors with a faculty of two: Mary Allen and Mary Gough. This building was razed in 1910 for a larger and more-modern structure. On June 15, 2007, the school closed its doors on a legacy of Catholic education and opened as the Charles Kelly School, part of the Upper Darby School District. (St. Charles Parish and Barbara McFadden.)

In 1874, William J. Kelly purchased four lots in Fernwood for $1,200. The first Fernwood School was built the next year at a cost of $6,000. It had one room on each floor, which was typical for that time. Additions were made in 1904. However, in 1923, a completely new building was constructed.

The Primos Public School was built in 1903 on land purchased from Joseph Bunting. It was located on Bunting Lane. This 1925 picture was taken when it was the only two-room schoolhouse still in use in Upper Darby. The building was later used as a community center. The Civic Association and the Girl Scouts of Primos-Secane held meetings there until it was destroyed by fire around 1970.

In 1909, part of Michael Burnley's farm was purchased to build Garrettford Elementary School. In February 1910, children paraded from the Central School on Burmont Road at School Lane to their new school at Garrett Road near Burmont Road. The original two buildings were raised in 1941 for the construction of the present grey stone building. The school opened in 1942. Elizabeth Kirk, a descendant of one of the original farm families, served as the principal from 1913 to 1947. Below, these Garrettford girls are in their domestic science class. The teacher is Dorothy Clymer. Note that the girl in the front is using a foot pedal sewing machine, and the girl to the left wears knee socks. They all have the then-popular bobbed hair style.

Aronimink, which means "the place of the beaver," was given its name by the Lenni-Lenape Indians. The land was part of the estate of Dr. George Smith. He served as state senator and his education committee wrote the 1836 bill providing public education in Pennsylvania. He was the first president of the Upper Darby School Board, serving in that position for 25 years. This school was built in 1938 to fulfill his wishes.

These second-grade children are lined up in front of the Keystone School in 1912. The architecture was very similar to the Primos School on page 104. The boy in the big bow tie, fourth from the right in the center row, is young Vanleer I. Bond. He later owned the Bond Department Store located in his brother Richard's shopping center at State Road and Lansdowne Avenue. Vanleer served many years on the Upper Darby School Board. The newer Keystone building is now the public safety building. (Dorothy Bond.)

These children sit proudly in front of the old Highland Park School in 1924. Burton England is in the third row, second from the left. England's wife, Mae, was a long-time contributor to the historical society. The teacher is Miss McCleech. The present open-space building was constructed in 1974. (Mae England.)

The Upper Darby Junior High School (presently Beverly Hills Middle School) opened on September 7, 1930, on the land of Brookfield Farm. The open space around the school was the Beverly Hills Golf Course. Below, First Lady Eleanor Roosevelt visits the school for a war bond concert on March 18, 1943. (William Elder.)

This 1951 picture of the previous Upper Darby High School shows Arlington Cemetery cherry blossoms in bloom. This building was constructed in 1919 and torn down in 1971. In the aerial view below is the high school with a smaller long building to its left. This was the original high school, later used for the administration offices. The central part of the school is the cafeteria and classrooms, built in 1950, and the left part is the gymnasium. In front of the cafeteria is Cartledge Memorials, and the house in the trees is the historic Evans House. In the foreground is Arlington Cemetery.

When Thurso, the home of Anthony J. Drexel Jr. was destroyed by fire in 1897, the property was purchased by the Catholic Archdiocese of Philadelphia. They built St. Vincent's Orphanage. In 1953, it was converted to Archbishop Prendergast High School for boys. In 1956, when Monsignor Bonner was built for boys next door, the original building became Archbishop Prendergast High School for girls. Today, Prendergast and Bonner remain separate schools but under the same administration. The carriage house from the Drexel estate is still there today (see page 39).

Seven

SERVICE TO THE PUBLIC

Benjamin Franklin was driven to improve the lives and conditions of the people. He was the first to install streetlights, grade the roads, and install a sewer system. He formed the first free public library and fire department and founded the University of Pennsylvania in 1740. These concepts soon spread to the nearest western suburb, Upper Darby.

Samuel and George Sellers from Derbyshire, England, the first permanent settlers, were inventors and innovators. It is said that Samuel was the first wire weaver in America. He and Anna Gibbons' marriage was the first held at the Darby Meeting, 1684. Coleman Sellers invented and built the first steam locomotive and the first movie projector c. 1834. In 1933, Sarah Sellers willed her family home to be used as Upper Darby's public library.

Other founding families—descendants from the original Swedish, Welsh, and English stock and, later, immigrants such as Italians, Irish, and Poles—were also instrumental in helping found the first public parks, hospitals, churches, and schools. Fire companies developed in different sections of the township, and the police department grew. Over time, civic organizations such as Scout groups, women's clubs, and Rotary were born. Upper Darby became a full-service township.

Fire apparatus of all descriptions furnished on the most approved plan.

This Hydraulion was an early fire apparatus manufactured by Sellers and Pennock of Philadelphia. In 1822, the Hydraulion was the first piece of fire apparatus with a suction hose and fittings to be put in use anywhere. With changes in technology, it became obsolete by 1840. (Delaware County Historical Society.)

Cardington-Stonehurst Fire Company No. 4 was chartered in 1916. Seen in this image from around 1930, firemen pose with two c. 1912 American LaFrance fire engines. The bell on the fire station is from the Burd Orphan Asylum and is housed as a memorial at the site today. (Keith Lockhart.)

The Primos-Secane and Westbrook Park Company No. 5, chartered in 1955, was the first Upper Darby Fire Company to purchase a snorkel apparatus. The men are pictured here with their 1939 American LaFrance fire truck. It was first stored in the rear of Burn Brae at Baltimore Pike and Oak Avenue. These firemen's coats were rubber, and their helmets were plastic. (Keith Lockhart.)

In January 1907, a group of citizens met at Sommer's Hall, and Garrettford Volunteer Fire Company No. 1 was born. It was chartered in 1917 and remains today as the only all-volunteer fire company in Upper Darby. The present brick building is at the same location on Edmonds Avenue. The ring on the pole, a Baldwin locomotive wheel rim, was struck as the alarm.

Celebrated photographer E. Clyde Eichholtz captured this funeral procession in about 1916 on Market Street (now Edmonds Avenue) in Garrettford, a part of Drexel Hill. The men of the Garrettford Fire Company honor one of their own.

On the Upper Darby High School football field are the five fire stations representing the Upper Darby Fire Department around 1940. In 1899, Highland Park Fire Company No. 2, chartered in 1911, decided to form a hose company. It was the first company to have lime-green apparatus. It had an open-rear rescue truck called the Pie Wagon, which is in the first row of vehicles, at the far right. (David Evans.)

Upper Darby Fire Company No. 3, chartered in 1916, covered the Sixty-ninth Street shopping district, at one time considered to be the county's highest-valued area. This picture was taken in front of the Elizabeth Manor Apartments at Brief Avenue and West Chester Pike in about 1926. (David Evans.)

Men of the police department show off their car in front of the terminal building on Market Street. This c. 1925 scene shows many people viewing Upper Darby Township's early car. The insignia on the side reads "Department of Police No. 1 UD Township." (Upper Darby Police Department.)

The Upper Darby Police Department is seen here on Baltimore Pike between First and Second Streets in 1912. From left to right, the men are (first row) Chief Louis Monsall, Obie Cain on the motorcycle, and Comdr. Frank Shea in the bowler hat; (second row) Dennis Logue, Jack Flemming, Charles Wakerman, Jack Duffy, and John Leighton, all on horses. (Upper Darby Police Department.)

This is the third and present Upper Darby Township Municipal Building dedicated on May 6, 1931, replacing the one built at the same location at Garrett Road and Long Lane in 1920. These Upper Darby police officers are seen in the 1950s with their vehicles. Below is Mayor Sonny Kane (right), presenting a certificate of commendation in January 1976. Sgt. Harry Collins was honored for his bravery in apprehending a robbery suspect near the Bond Shopping Center. On the left is Police Chief Joseph Charley. In 1971, Upper Darby voted on a home rule type of government providing for a mayor to preside over the township council. Sonny Kane was elected the first mayor. (Both, Upper Darby Police Department.)

The Upper Darby police color guard officiated at township ceremonies, parades, and funerals. Pictured around 1980 are, from left to right, Warren Chambers, William R. Johnson, Ike Eisenhouth, George Crowley, John Berry, William Devine, Andrew Gallagher, James Kenny, John Nee, Bill Myers, Jack Perry, and Edward Crawford. (Upper Darby Police Department.)

In 1975, Upper Darby had a K-9 Unit operating in the township. Seen here with police superintendent Joseph Charley (center) are, from left to right, Donald Gabe with Duke, badge No. 4; Joseph Zambone with Pax, badge No. 1; William R. Johnson with Nicky, badge No. 3; and James Kenney with Barron, badge No. 2. (William R. Johnson.)

Upper Darby mounted police returned to the Upper Darby police force in the 1970s. Ronald Dewees hands over the reins of his horse Amigo to mounted patrolman Warren Chambers. (Upper Darby Police Department.)

This motorcycle unit was lined up behind the public safety building on West Chester Pike in 1974. Seen here from left to right are Joseph Dougherty, Mark Nestel, Keven Dougherty, Sgt. Joseph Helyenick, Brian Duffy, Lou Gentile, Thomas Sharp, John Cunningham, and Timothy Law. (Upper Darby Police Department.)

This police unit marches proudly down the unit block of Garrett Road, approaching Market Street in the 1925 Memorial Day parade. The large stone building is currently the Wells Fargo bank building.

The Upper Darby Police Strike Force Anti-Crime Unit also worked undercover in the 1970s with long hair, beards, and old clothes. The second from the left is Paul Schneider. (Upper Darby Police Department.)

The public safety building took over the Keystone School, constructed in 1923. It replaced the original school that was erected in 1875 and still stands next to it. Today, this building holds the police department, the records office, and a courtroom. (Upper Darby Police Department.)

Sarah Sellers died in June 1933, leaving her home, Hoodland, and money for library purposes. In 1930, a library committee was established to discuss plans for opening a library in Upper Darby. The library occupied several buildings before the Sellers house was renovated in June 1935 and formally named the Sellers Memorial Free Public Library. In 1957, the grounds and building were officially transferred to Upper Darby Township. In December 1975, the Patrick J. Martin Memorial wing was dedicated. Part of this brick building can be seen on the right. (Sellers Memorial Library.)

The bookmobile of the Sellers Memorial Library first appeared in July 1947 as a station wagon visiting summer playgrounds. In 1953, a trailer was added through the efforts of August Niemeyer to house additional books. In 1967, a custom-made vehicle that held 4,000 volumes was purchased. By June 30, 1983, the bookmobile service ceased operation due to the change in usage patterns of patrons. The custom truck below, c. 1972, is seen with librarians and staff in front. The last bookmobile librarians were Mary Alice (Mally) Clark and Marion Jones. (Sellers Memorial Library.)

The early Swedish cabin stands at the end of Creek Road on Darby Creek. In 1944, Upper Darby Township presented it to the Girl Scouts of Delaware County. Pictured here are members of the Brownie troop. In the front row, second from the left, is Dorothy B. "Debe" Hill. In the 1980s, she was one of the founders of the Upper Darby Historical Society and an advocate until her death in 1996. (Dorothy B. "Debe" Hill.)

Senator Edwin B. "Ted" Erickson has served the Upper Darby community since 1976. His first experience in government was as the chief administrative officer for Upper Darby Township. Prior to being elected state senator in 2001, he served on the Delaware County Council, and for nine years, he was the executive director of Delaware County, overseeing government operations in one of the largest-populated counties in the commonwealth. (Senator Erickson.)

The Llanerch Women's Club took a trip to Washington, DC, in October 1973. They are seen here on the steps of the Capitol building. The club, part of the General Federation of Women's Clubs, was made up of women from Upper Darby and Haverford. In the front, wearing the white coat with black purse, is Mae England of Upper Darby, who hosted many meetings in her home. On the right side of the top row is Lillian Griffin, also of Upper Darby. (Mary Courtney of Haverford Historical Society.)

Ruth Schlosman, left, was employed by the Kellett Company and trained in riveting at a special class set up in the metal shop of Upper Darby High School. Kellett rented the Gulf Building on Lansdowne Avenue, just two blocks north of State Road. Behind the building, Kellett tested autogyros and early helicopters for the Piasecki Corporation. Schlosman was paid $25 per week to manufacture ailerons for the P49 airplane. She was the "gunner" with a rivet gun, and another woman was the "bucker" who flattened the rivets with a heavy piece of metal. She told stories of going to Sixty-ninth Street with groups of workers after their shift at midnight to such places as Chez Vous and Glendennings. The businesses stayed open all night during the war to accommodate industrial workers' shifts. The plant closed a short time after the war ended in 1945.

US Marines are pictured in front of their headquarters building at 1026 Providence Road in the Secane section of Upper Darby on a Memorial Day celebration in 2010. They have leased the building from Upper Darby Township for approximately 12 years and have done extensive restoration. There is a carriage house and springhouse on the property. In 1870, it was owned by J.W. Ash and was part of the Greenbank Farm area. (Upper Darby Marine Corps League.)

The members of the board of the Upper Darby Historical Society are photographed for their 10th anniversary. They are, from left to right, (first row) Mary Ellen Scott, Dorothy "Debe" Hill, Catherine Mitchell, Beverly Rorer, Frances Long, and Margaret F. Johnson; (second row) Louis Fiorito, Kathleen Clarke, William McDevitt, Alan Neary, Fred Bencker, and David Andrews.

Visit us at
arcadiapublishing.com

www.ingramcontent.com/pod-product-compliance
Lightning Source LLC
Chambersburg PA
CBHW050605110426
42813CB00008B/2468